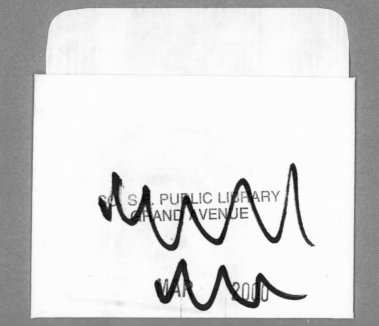

# Carnaval

# George Ancona

H A R C O U R T   B R A C E   &   C O M P A N Y        *San Diego   New York   London*

Requests for permission to make copies of any part of the work should
be mailed to: Permissions Department, Harcourt Brace & Company,
6277 Sea Harbor Drive, Orlando, Florida 32887-6777.

Text set in Adroit Medium   Display type set in Remedy Double Extras
Designed by George Ancona and Camilla Filancia

First edition   F E D C B A   A B C D E F (pb)

Library of Congress Cataloging-in-Publication Data
Ancona, George.
Carnaval / George Ancona.
p. cm
Summary: Text and photographs present the traditions and rituals
of the annual celebration of Carnaval as experienced in the small
Brazilian city of Olinda.
ISBN 0-15-201793-3   ISBN 0-15-201792-5 (pb)
1. Carnival–Brazil–Olinda–Juvenile literature.   2. Olinda (Brazil)–Social
life and customs–Juvenile literature. [1. Carnival–Brazil.  2. Festivals–
Brazil.  3. Holidays–Brazil.  4. Brazil–Social life and customs.]  I. Title.
GT4233.O55A53   1999
394.26981´34–dc21      98-47297

**Printed in Singapore**

*To the people of Olinda, com muitos abraços*

*Muito obrigado—*
Thanks to all the people whose friendship and hospitality made this book possible. To Katarina Real, who reviewed the manuscript; to Sílvio Botelho, Helena Carvalhosa, and Wanderly Antunes Bezerra, director of the Olinda Tourist Office; to Olimpio Bonald Neto, Marcia Marcondes, Maristela Lacerda, Dona Maria, Paulo de Souza, *Mestre* Salustiano, and the Grupo Comunidade Assumnido Suas Crianças; to Meia Noite, Afonjah, Janaina and Marcia Lince, Aurinha do Côco, and the family of Julião das Máscaras; to Nilson and Adjairo Cabral, Rosinha Bezerra and Almir Campos, Flávio Palhaço Arco-Iris, Agamenon, and Walter; and finally, to my wife, Helga, whose knowledge of Brazil and Portuguese helped us find our way to the people we met, and my daughter Marina, who assisted me with the photography.

**t**he people of the city of Olinda say that theirs is the best *carnaval* in Brazil. *Carnaval* is a five-day festival of music, dance, and play that takes place just before the Christian season of Lent. Preparations begin in January and continue right up to the celebration at the end of February.

In the days before *carnaval*, the everyday sounds of crowing roosters and ringing church bells mix with the pounding of drums and the music of brass bands.

February is summer in Brazil, and it is very hot. But despite the heat, the townsfolk are bustling about getting ready. *Carnaval* celebrates the three main cultures of Brazil: indigenous, European, and African. All three can be seen in the songs and dances that children and teenagers practice in the afternoons.

For many weeks Dona Maria has been sewing costumes for the neighborhood children. Parents come to help sew sequins and ruffles on the bright fabrics. Gradually the house fills with children trying on their costumes.

Maristela is an artist who creates masks made of papier-mâché, pieces of paper dipped in a flour paste. When the masks are dry, Maristela paints them with designs and adds decorations of feathers and ribbons. Her masks cover part or all of the face.

Other masks cover the entire head. *Mestre* (master) Paulo is busy painting bull masks. The bull, like the rooster and the bear, is a carnival mask based on myths from northeastern Brazil. When he finishes painting them, *Mestre* Paulo puts the masks out in the sun to dry.

The streets of Olinda are too narrow for the large floats used in the big cities. Instead, *bonecos gigantes,* or giant puppets, are carried through the town. Olinda has become famous for these puppets. Sílvio Botelho is the best-known maker of giant puppets in Olinda.

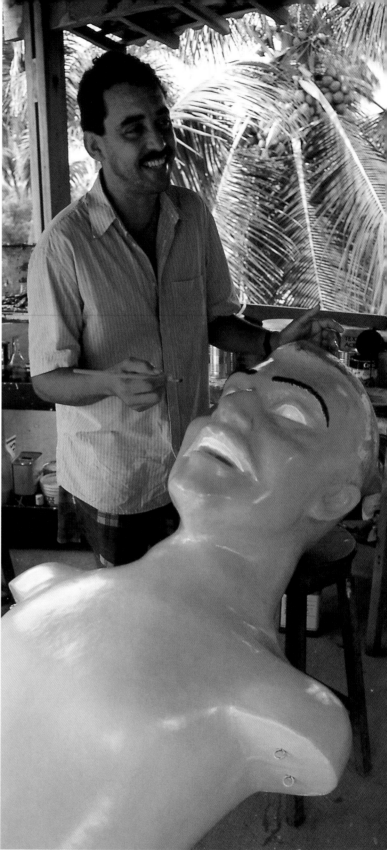

*Mestre* Sílvio first carves the head and hands out of Styrofoam. Then he covers them with papier-mâché. When the paper is dry, he glues the head to the body, and covers everything with fiberglass. After it is painted, he attaches the arms.

Sílvio's assistants then put hair on the puppet's head.

Sometimes, in the crush of people during *carnaval*, a puppet is dropped. An apprentice repairs the damage a puppet has suffered.

The first puppet, *O Homem da Meia-Noite*, the Midnight Man, was made more than sixty years ago. With his top hat and gold tooth, he has become the symbol of Olinda's *carnaval*.

After a few years, the townsfolk worried that the Midnight Man was lonely, so they made him a wife. She, too, sports a gold tooth. She is called *A Mulher do Dia*, the Woman of the Day. The two

were married in a midnight ceremony in front of a church. The entire town attended.

Since the father was night and the mother day, when the children were made they were named *A Menina da Tarde,* the Girl of the Afternoon, and *O Menino da Tarde,* the Boy of the Afternoon.

It is a Friday night, a few weeks before *carnaval*. People gather in the plazas to play and sing traditional *carnaval* songs.

When a crowd is assembled, the musicians lead the singers on a serenade through the town. These spontaneous parades are called *serenatas*. Even though *carnaval* is still weeks ahead, the partying gains momentum each day.

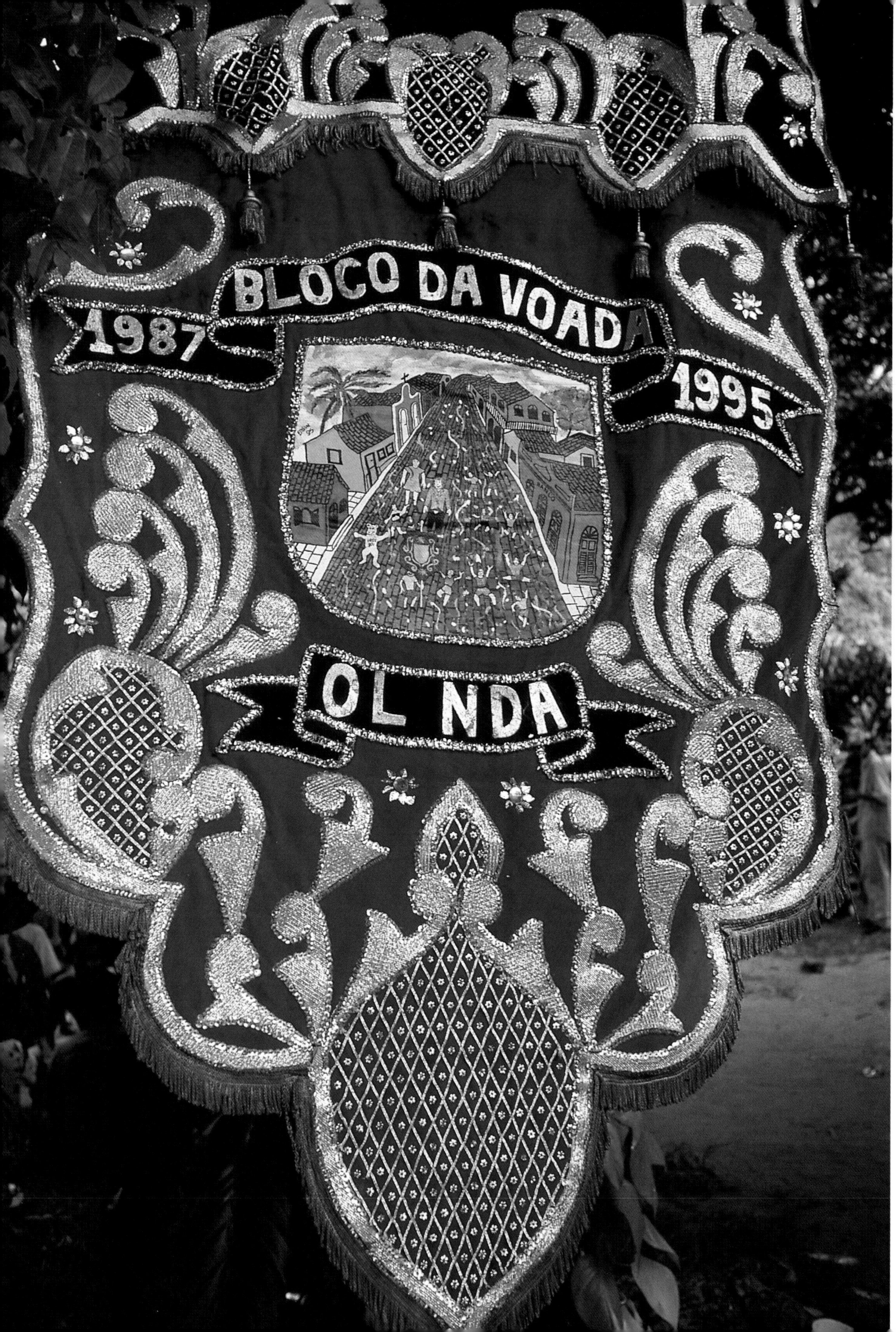
BLOCO DA VOADA
1987
1995
OL NDA

For *carnaval,* every neighbor-hood forms a parade group called a *bloco,* with its own name, colors, band, and costumes. Everyone in the *bloco* follows behind the neighborhood banner, called an *estandarte.*

The *blocos* are named for legends, funny phrases, or famous local people such as the waiter who was nicknamed *Batata* (Potato). Since Batata had to work during *carnaval,* he would celebrate on Ash Wednesday by inviting friends to eat tasty codfish and potatoes on the beach. His friends formed a *bloco* and had a puppet made in his honor.

Although there are many dances and rhythms in the Northeast, two that are often danced for *carnaval* are the *frevo* and the *maracatu*.

The *maracatu* is danced to the rhythm of drums and other percussion instruments. African slaves created the *maracatu* during Brazil's colonial period. Children rehearse this dance, which celebrates the coronation of an African king.

In a community center, children try on their costumes and practice the *frevo*. This dance grew out of marches of military bands. Barefoot dancers with rolled-up pants would leap and perform acrobatic steps while marching with the bands. The little umbrella is a tradition that recalls the people of the Northeast, who walked and rode with an umbrella to protect them from the hot sun and strong rains.

By Friday, the first day of *carnaval*, the population of Olinda has grown by the thousands with tourists who have come from all over the world.

Townspeople and visitors put on their costumes, masks, and wigs, and paint their faces. *Carnaval* gives people the chance to become somebody different. For the next five days and nights the people of Olinda and their visitors forget their troubles and give themselves over to the music, dance, and the joy of *carnaval*.

This is a night of splendor. A parade led by the *Homem da Meia-Noite* slowly works its way through the merry crowd. *Frevo* dancers in colorful costumes lead the brass bands along the streets. The dancers leap and spin as they toss the tiny twirling umbrella from hand to hand and between their legs. The umbrella helps them keep their balance.

The word *frevo* is short for the Portuguese word *ferver*, "to boil."
And the dancers do seem to boil in the heat of the night and
the music. Soon even the bystanders are swept up and join in the
dance. The revelry lasts all through the night till the early hours
of Saturday morning.

The next morning forty *bonecos* wait outside of *Mestre Sílvio's* house. The music starts. The puppets are raised onto the heads of young men who are called the "souls" of the puppets because they give them life. Hidden by the puppets' huge trousers or skirts, the men peek through an opening to find their way. As the musicians move down the street, the towering puppets lurch and begin to dance their way into the parade.

The puppets are characters from stories and from the town. Among them are the Devil, the Fat Lady, the Crazy Beauty, Yvonne the Fortune-teller, Maria of the Full Moon, the Newsboy, the Photographer, and there is even a John Travolta!

The bright summer sun shines on a sea of vivid costumes. Groups of teenage boys roam the streets dressed in clown costumes and women's masks. For laughs, they imitate the fancy masked ladies of the Spanish and Venetian carnivals. As they walk along, they play clacking castanets, an influence of the Spanish in Brazil.

An elderly gentleman, nicknamed "the Lord," strolls down the street in top hat and frock coat, carrying an umbrella. Years ago his father inherited the suit from his boss and began to use it for *carnaval*. Now he wears the suit and continues his father's tradition.

Mornings during *carnaval* are for the children. Costumed parents and children join their *blocos* for the parades. Those who are too small to walk are carried on their parent's shoulders.

Every day new *blocos* take to
the streets. Some people change
costumes daily in order to be
part of a different *bloco*. This
Sunday morning many families
arrive wearing the *burrinha*,
the little donkey costume. The
*burrinha* hangs by suspenders
from the shoulders of the rider.
The donkey wobbles back and
forth when the rider pulls on
the reins.

Another popular *carnaval* figure is the bull, *bumba-meu-boi,* a traditional figure in stories and plays of the Northeast.

The *urso,* or bear, is also an old carnival costume. Sometimes it is held by a chain. It invokes the dancing bears of European gypsies who traveled from town to town.

By the afternoons the streets are clogged with happy people. Since there are no barriers, the crowds merge with the bands and dancers as everyone makes their way through the streets.

A booming of drums announces the arrival
of one of the many *blocos* that dances the
*maracatu*. Ladies-in-waiting accompany
the king and queen and other members
of an African royal court. The regal pair
is shielded from the sun by a ceremonial
umbrella. Surrounding the group are
warriors in feathered headdresses who
represent the native peoples of Brazil.

Some of the ladies-in-waiting carry a doll dressed the same as themselves. This is *Calunga,* a sacred figure that is said to hold magical powers that protect the *maracatu* group.

There are many groups of *maracatus.* On one street there may be a *bloco* of children, while a few blocks away an adult *maracatu* makes its way through the crowds. All over town, scores of drummers fill the air with thunder to announce the arrival of each elegantly dressed monarch and his court.

On Sunday the outer neighborhoods of Olinda celebrate *carnaval* with the *maracatu rural*. Many years ago, the slaves who worked on the sugarcane plantations in the countryside combined their African traditions with those of the native peoples and made the *maracatu* their own.

The soldiers are called *caboclos* and wear a headdress of strands of colored cellophane that looks like a lion's mane. Their broad-shouldered capes have intricate designs of sequins. Under the capes are three immense bells that clang as the men dance. The *caboclos* carry beribboned spears that they thrust and twirl as they open the way for the procession. They look like an army of fierce warriors.

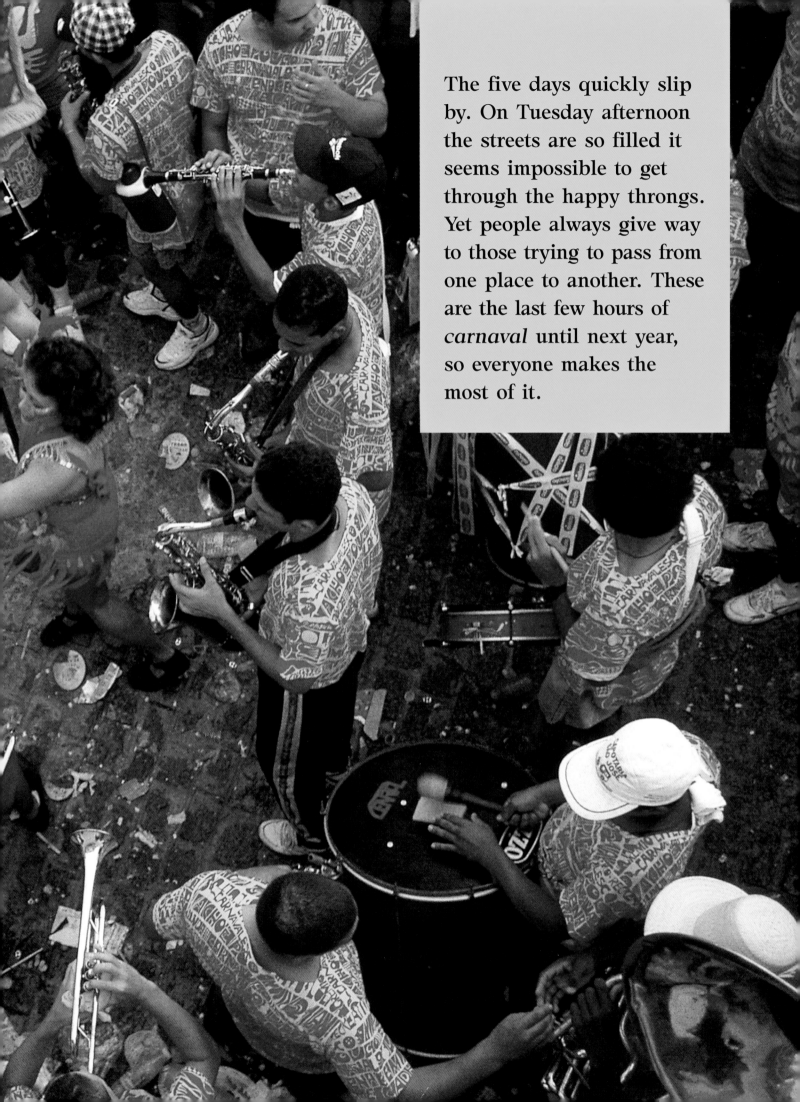

The five days quickly slip by. On Tuesday afternoon the streets are so filled it seems impossible to get through the happy throngs. Yet people always give way to those trying to pass from one place to another. These are the last few hours of *carnaval* until next year, so everyone makes the most of it.

As the sun rises on Ash Wednesday the streets are quiet. The church bells ring, summoning the sleepy merrymakers of yesterday to mass. Officially *carnaval* is over. Tired visitors begin to leave Olinda. Most people are back at work, but there are still some who will continue the *carnaval* into the weekend. One tireless *bloco* bears the name, *Pa'rou, porque?!* (Why stop?!) It's hard to stop when you're having so

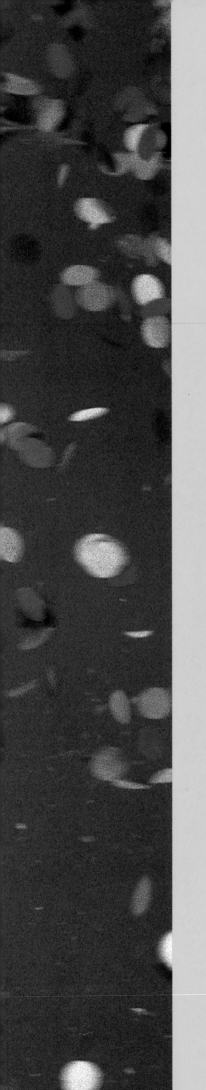

# Note from the Author

**O**linda, with its colonial architecture and winding cobblestone streets, is in northeastern Brazil. In 1531 when the Portuguese explorer Duarte Coelho Pereira first saw the green-covered hills of what is now Brazil, he exclaimed, *"Ó linda situação para uma vila!"* (Oh, what a beautiful place for a town!)

When the Portuguese settlers built the town they named it Olinda, "how beautiful." Today the old colonial town overlooks the ocean and the modern city of Recife.

*Carnaval* is celebrated all over Brazil. The biggest parades are in the cities of Rio de Janeiro, Recife, and Salvador, but Olinda's *carnaval* is unique. Olinda is a small town and its *carnaval* includes more of the folk-lore, music, and traditions of the northeast region of Brazil. There are no grandstands for spectators—everyone joins the parades. For five days the streets are filled with thousands of laughing, singing, and dancing people.

In Europe, carnival is a celebration of the return of spring and takes place during the five days before Ash Wednesday, which marks the beginning of the Christian season of Lent, the forty days of fasting and penance before Easter. In Brazil *carnaval* also takes place before Ash Wednesday, though because of the seasonal differences the celebration occurs at the end of summer.

The Europeans brought carnival to the Americas, where each new country changed it to make the celebration its own. In Brazil the early Portuguese settlers wore disguises and threw eggshells filled with perfumed water at each other. Nowadays the celebration has become much more elaborate.

But wherever carnival is celebrated—be it in Europe, the Caribbean, Latin America, or Mardi Gras in New Orleans—it is a time for fun and joy.